Jesus is Born

D0417091

To my parents, Doreen and Patrick Gilbert,
for all their love and encouragement
A. Y. G.

Text by Sophie Piper
Illustrations copyright © 2015 Anne Yvonne Gilbert
This edition copyright © 2015 Lion Hudson

The right of Anne Yvonne Gilbert to be identified as the illustrator
of this work has been asserted by her in accordance with the
Copyright, Designs and Patents Act 1988.

All rights reserved. No part of this publication may be reproduced or
transmitted in any form or by any means, electronic or mechanical,
including photocopy, recording, or any information storage and
retrieval system, without permission in writing from the publisher.

Published by Lion Children's Books
an imprint of
Lion Hudson plc
Wilkinson House, Jordan Hill Road,
Oxford OX2 8DR, England
www.lionhudson.com/lionchildrens

ISBN 978 0 7459 6521 5

First edition 2015

A catalogue record for this book is available from the British Library

Printed and bound in Malaysia, July 2015, LH18

**Waltham Forest
Libraries**

904 000 00603705	
Askews & Holts	01-Dec-2017
C220.95 PIP	£6.99
5583362	

Jesus *is* Born

Retold by Sophie Piper

Illustrated by Anne Yvonne Gilbert

LION
CHILDREN'S

The story of the first Christmas has been told and retold for some 2000 years. From the Gospel of Luke, in the Bible, we know this story:

In the little town of Nazareth, in Galilee, lived a young woman named Mary. She had promised to marry a man named Joseph, and the wedding was not far off.

Then God sent the angel Gabriel with a message for her. Mary gasped in fear at the sight of the heavenly being.

"Don't be afraid," said the angel. "God has chosen you to be the mother of his Son. You will name him 'Jesus'. He will bring God's blessing to the world."

Mary was astonished. "That can't be true!" she replied. "I can't be a mother before I'm even married."

"With God, all things are possible," replied the angel.

Mary bowed her head. "I will do as God wants," she replied.

It was not long after that another messenger came to Nazareth. This second one was sent by the Roman emperor who ruled the land.

"Everyone must go to their home town," he declared. "They must enter their names on a list of taxpayers. The emperor demands taxes from everyone."

It so happened that Joseph's home town was Bethlehem. "We will go there together," he told his bride-to-be. "For you and the baby you are expecting will be my new family."

Of course, there were many people going to Bethlehem for the same reason as Joseph. When he and Mary reached the town, there was no room left in the inn.

The couple had to shelter in a stable. There, where a donkey shuffled and an ox slowly munched, Mary's child, God's only Son, was born.

On the hills nearby, some shepherds were out watching their sheep through the dark and danger of the night.

Suddenly an angel appeared.

"I bring good news!" cried the brightly shining figure. "Tonight, in Bethlehem, a child has been born: God's chosen king.

"He is the one who will rescue you from all your woes!

"He is the one who will bring God's blessing to the world.

"Yet tonight the newborn sleeps in Bethlehem,

wrapped in swaddling clothes,

cradled in a manger."

Then the sky was filled
with angels, all singing,
"Glory to God in heaven;
On earth, peace."

All at once the sky went dark.
The shepherds were astonished.
Had they all been dreaming?
Or had they really seen
angels, and was the message true?
    They hurried off to the
darkened streets of Bethlehem.

But where should they look?

A glimmer of light led them to a tiny room where they found Joseph and Mary and the baby, just as the angel had said.

Mary's eyes sparkled with joy as they told their news.

Not many miles away, in the city of Jerusalem, another story was about to unfold: a story we know from the Gospel of Matthew, in the Bible.

In the royal palace there lived a man named Herod, who ruled the land around on behalf of the Roman emperor. He had heard troubling news. Strangers had come to the city from lands to the east, and they said they were looking for a newborn king.

"We study the night sky for signs," they explained. "When we saw a new star, we believed it was a sign that a king had been born to your people, the Jews."

Herod was not a godly man, but he knew the stories at the heart of the Jewish faith: that one day God would send a king as great as their greatest king of days gone by – a king like David. He wanted no such rival to his power!

Accordingly he summoned the chief priests: "This ancient promise of God sending a king," he said. "Remind me what the stories tell us: where will he be born?"

"In Bethlehem," replied the priests, "the very place where King David was born."

Herod smiled grimly as he made a secret plan.

"If any child is being set up as a rival king, I will get rid of him," he said. "I'll send those strangers to find out who it is."

As those same strangers were directed to the Bethlehem road, the new star shone on their way. It led them to the hilltop town, and the very house where Mary was, with her son Jesus.

They brought out their tribute gifts:
gold, frankincense,
and myrrh.

That night, in a dream, an angel spoke to them.
"Do not go back to King Herod. He means
to harm the child."
They returned to their home country
by a different route.

In a dream an angel also spoke to Joseph.

"Beware: King Herod will soon send soldiers to Bethlehem to kill any child who might grow up to believe himself king.

"Get up now, while it is night, and take Mary and Jesus to faraway Egypt.

"For Mary's child Jesus is God's own Son; and you must keep him safe.

"When he grows up, he will bring God's blessing to the world."

Other titles from Lion Children's Books

On That Christmas Night   *Lois Rock & Alison Jay*
The Animals' Christmas   *Elena Pasquali & Giuliano Ferri*
The Story of Christmas   *Mary Joslin & Alida Massari*
The Story of the Nativity   *Elena Pasquali & Sophie Windham*